Lerner SPORTS ROOKIE

SOCCER MANIA

MOST INCREDIBLE SOCCER MOMENTS

Cara Krenn

Lerner Publications ◆ Minneapolis

Lerner Publications Company
An imprint of Lerner Publishing Group, Inc.
241 First Avenue North
Minneapolis, MN 55401 USA

For reading levels and more information, look up this title at www.lernerbooks.com.

Main body text set in Mikado. Typeface provided by HVD fonts.

Editor: Evan Villas **Designer:** Viet Chu
Lerner team: Sue Marquis

Library of Congress Cataloging-in-Publication Data

Names: Krenn, Cara, author.
Title: Most incredible soccer moments / Cara Krenn.
Description: Minneapolis, MN : Lerner Publications, [2026] | Series: Soccer mania (Lerner sports rookie) | Includes bibliographical references and index. | Audience: Ages 5–8 | Audience: Grades K–1 | Summary: “One shot to win it all! Readers discover the most exhilarating goals, breathtaking saves, and historic wins in the history of professional soccer”— Provided by publisher.
Identifiers: LCCN 2024037174 (print) | LCCN 2024037175 (ebook) | ISBN 9798765668399 (library binding) | ISBN 9798765683743 (paperback) | ISBN 9798765681176 (epub)
Subjects: LCSH: Soccer—Juvenile literature.
Classification: LCC GV943.25 .K74 2026 (print) | LCC GV943.25 (ebook) | DDC 796.334—dc23/eng/20240813

LC record available at https://lccn.loc.gov/2024037174
LC ebook record available at https://lccn.loc.gov/2024037175

Manufactured in the United States of America
1-1011710-53807-1/21/2025

Table of Contents

What a Save!

Alisson Becker dives
for the ball. Wow!

Alisson Becker

Soccer is exciting! The best soccer moments make fans cheer.

INSIDE SOCCER

Brazil has the most men's World Cup wins. The US has won the most women's World Cups.

Brazil beat Italy to win the 1970 men's World Cup. Brazil's last goal was one of the best team goals ever.

Almost every player helped. Carlos Alberto scored after a pass from Pelé.

Carlos Alberto
tivo... conciso... así es
Contac X
YARDLEY
MAJESTIC
Zaga
Pelikan
EL HERALDO

Argentina beat England in the 1986 men's World Cup. Diego Maradona scored the first goal with his hand.

Players can't use their hands. English fans were mad! Later in the game, Maradona dribbled past many players to score again.

Diego Maradona

The final match of the 1999 women's World Cup was tied. The game ended in penalty kicks.

US goalie Briana Scurry made a big save. Brandi Chastain's kick broke the tie. The US beat China.

INSIDE SOCCER

A penalty kick is a free kick in front of the goal. It happens when a player is fouled or to break a tie.

Carli Lloyd scored a hat trick in 16 minutes during the 2015 women's World Cup final. It was the fastest ever in a World Cup. The US beat Japan.

INSIDE SOCCER

A hat trick is when a player scores three goals in one game.

The US was losing to Brazil in the 2011 women's World Cup. Megan Rapinoe crossed the ball. Then Abby Wambach hit it into the net.

The game went to penalty kicks. The US won.

WAMBACH
20
Abby Wambach
USA

Japan won the 2011 women's World Cup after an earthquake harmed the country. The win was special to Japan.

Homare Sawa

The 2022 men's World Cup final was close. Lionel Messi scored two of Argentina's three goals.

France's Kylian Mbappé scored a hat trick to tie the game. Argentina won in penalty kicks.

Lionel Messi

Soccer is super exciting for fans!
What will be the next great moment?

adidas
adidas
adidas
adidas

Glossary

cross: to pass the ball across the field

dribble: to move the ball with your feet

earthquake: when part of the earth shakes

Learn More

Buckley, James, Jr. *Perfect Penalty Kick!: The U.S. Women's Soccer Team at the 1999 World Cup*. Minneapolis: Bearport, 2024.

Leed, Percy. *Soccer's World Cup*. Minneapolis: Lerner Publications, 2025.

Wagner, Zelda. *Soccer Superstars*. Minneapolis: Lerner Publications, 2025.

Index

Photo Acknowledgments

Image credits: Laurence Griffiths/Getty Images, p. 5; Mark Leech/Offside/Getty Images, p. 7; Popperfoto/Getty Images, p. 9; Paul Bereswill/Getty Images, p. 11; AP Photo/Eric Risberg, p. 13; Dennis Grombkowski/Getty Images, p. 15; Alex Livesey/FIFA via Getty Images, p. 17; Alex Grimm/Getty Images, p. 19; Anne-Christine Poujoulat/AFP via Getty Images, p. 21; Pedro Pardo/AFP via Getty Images, p. 23.

Cover: Matt Jacques/Alamy Live News.
Design elements: vid64/Getty Images; boytaro Thongbun/500px/Getty Images.